# The Only Truth is Love.
# A Journey of Love, Loss and Hope Through Poetry.

RENATO PETRONIO

ISBN-10: 0-9946005-1-8
ISBN-13: 978-0-9946005-1-6
Publisher: Renato Petronio
Editor: Julia Petronio
At time of publication this book is also available through Amazon as an ebook

# DEDICATION

In loving memory of my wife Andrea Jane Leys Petronio

I will always miss you
I shall miss you unto my last breath
Always in my heart my love x

# CONTENTS

# ACKNOWLEDGMENTS

I thank the following friends and family for your support, guidance and comfort during my wife Andrea, daughter Julia and my trials. Our friends, Jenny, Lisa, Audrey, Tony and Sam. Janene and Damien. Renae. Jo and her family. Liz and Marcus. Debbie and Harvey. Ava and Ross. Gerry. Wayne. Our family, Henry, Jo and their family. My brother Richard, sister Serena and niece Michelle. Our family in Italy. Our beautiful doggies who loved Andrea unconditionally. Our beautiful daughter Julia, who for Andrea and I shall always be our greatest blessing. The Lord Jesus Christ, who waits to bring you home my love x

"The path of sorrow and that path alone, leads to the

land where sorrow is unknown" (William Cowper)

Psalm 34 : 18

"The LORD is near to the broken hearted and saves the crushed in spirit."

Matthew 5 : 4

4 "Blessed are those who mourn, for they shall be comforted."

# PREFACE

The depth of one's love is realised when one grieves. A simple yet terrible statement for those of us who weep.

I have written this book as a testimony of myself and my daughters, friends and family's love for Andrea our wife, mother and friend; we will miss you till our last breath.

I never intended to write a book of poetry, or for that matter ever thought I would have the strength or desire to do so. After many years of writing as a way of dealing with sorrow, I feel I should tell our story. All grief is different, so I hope this book helps those in darkness, in a very small degree find a way through.

If we love we will grieve, there is no escape. From my writings you will see that I believe in Jesus Christ, He showed Himself to me during my darkest dark, if it were not so, I would not be here today.

Please seek help if your darkness is too great, there are beautiful people in this world that will rush to you like a running stream.

There is both darkness and light within these pages, as both must be travelled. Try and be kind and gentle to yourself during your darkness.

I hope with time you reach your light, wherever that may be.

Always in my heart my love x

# Thankyou

## 1. Time up *by Andrea Jane Leys Petronio (6th March 2013)*

Winds blow and leaves rustle,
I stand and look to the sky.
God has now made my path clear,
A painful but graceful road to follow.

May sunshine glow from my face in my final days,
And family and friends not dwell nor shed too many a tear.
But bid me goodbye with singing and laughter,
And memories of our time long together.


My darling Janey girl, rest now and wait for gentle Christ.
Your loving husband Renato and beautiful daughter Julia.
(† 3rd October 2013 age 46).

## 2. Poems of dark poems of light

Poems of dark poems of light,
Poems of grief all through the night.

Poems of sadness poems of fright,
When others sleep I seek the light.

Poems of loss poems of love,
I write them for you in Heaven above. x

## 3. The purpose of one's soul

The purpose of one's soul is to love, to give and receive love,
And the vehicle for that is one's heart.
That is why we need an open and loving heart,
For without this there is nothing.

For love is all there is,
All else is but a passing breeze.
Love is all He asks of us.

It's all there is,
All there was,
All there will ever be.

So love, feed your soul,
For this veil of tears will pass and in its place love.
For love is everlasting, before time and space, before thought,
So shall it be after all these things have passed.
Love will never fail. x

## 4. Rise like the Phoenix

Rise like the phoenix from the ashes of the sun,
For the world it needs lover's, poet's, dreamers every one.
Let your spirit soar above the clouds that others only see,
Let it rise to bring light and hope of His promise of eternity.

Let the spirits of your ancestor's surround and whisper in
your ear,
All the treasures of life's mysteries that others long to hear.
Let your smile beacon questions of what we truly seek,
For in these words are the treasures that my heart can only speak.

For you hear me speak of love and loss but do not fear
these things,
For in loss love rushes back to God, to wait for His
beautiful loving King.
I have loved so 'tis of His hand that I write of these things,
For He pours an endless everlasting flow, as I am filled to
my hearts brim.

Of love for love is love enough and love is love alone,
For all else is but a passing breeze and only love can lead
you home.
So drink from this cup of words and take up your fill,
For when love enters your unending soul, only then can it
be stilled.

For it seeks only love itself to fill itself with grace,
For its journey it must make in time back, to His everlasting
loving place.
Yes, I have loved and therefore cannot stop for 'tis the only
real truth,
That He gives from His heart to us to share, His love for me
and you. x

## 5. You are Heaven sent

You are Heaven sent you truly be,
From me to you I thank thee.
You tend the sick the frail the old,
Your gentle hearts they do not fold.

With gentle hearts you comfort soul.

My thanks to thee for your loving touch,
My wife you tended helped so much.
In Heaven God did ask the angels there,
Which of thee will give up eternity,
To be the kindness you all be.

These angels you were who gave so much,
And now here you stand as flesh and blood,
To grow old helping those in need,
To grow old helping those who bleed.

Know this from me to you,
That you are kind and just and true,
You help the sick without complaint,
You shield their hearts with the love you paint.

In your hearts you should know,
A life thus spent as you grow old,
Is worthy of such a story told.

In your hearts you should know,
My knee does bend for you it folds,
On bended knee my thanks to thee,
A life thus spent worthy of eternity.
(My thanks to the staff at St Vincent's Lismore for caring
for Andrea x)

# 6. There are people who travel in the day

There are people who travel in the day,
People who travel in the night.
There are people who run from your fears,
And others that hold you tight.

We thank God for the beautiful people,
The beacons He sent that night.
We thank those beautiful people,
Who held us oh so tight. x

# We stand in the fire

## 7. I shall never forget this day

I shall never forget this day, burnt, etched,
with sharpened claws upon my heart.
I shall never forget this day, the day my world was torn apart.
I shall never forget this day, the day for your loss to start.
I shall never forget this day, my mother and you to part.
I shall never forget this day, we would one day soon be apart.
I shall never forget this day.
I shall never forget this day.
I shall never forget this day.

# 8. I have loved you.

I have loved you in the morning in the newness of the light,
For we have finally beat this demon we have beat it won
the fight.
Its claws have loosened fallen it has shriveled before the light,
It has run away yelping as we beat it's back in flight.

The day now calm and peaceful with the brightest
warming light,
We hold each other close now in this wondrous warm
bright light.
No clouds now mask our future no clouds shut out the light,
The morn it has come for us, the morn what a beautiful sight. x

## 9. Adam and Eve born anew

Poems from my husband…
"Adam and Eve born anew" - written November 2012

We awaken are born like Adam and Eve,
Dragged through hell now to Heaven conceived.
Our eyelids flutter as light shines through,
A new day born for me and you.

I turn my head and you are there,
Softly laying on Heavens stair.
The angels stoop to gently hold,
Your body frail your body cold.
I stare at them burn through their souls,
They turn away cannot behold,
My love for thee a fire tall.

I hold you close and kiss your lips,
Your soul 'tis filled with my fiery breath.
They turn away and bow to you,
My love for thee is right and true.

My tears I wail and hold you tight,
I kiss your lips your soul ignites.
You draw your breath like a hurricane spawn,
Leaves of forests shake and fall.
Waves are formed in oceans tall,
Then breath out again, a new day dawns, a new day dawns.

We stand up tall Heaven's gate now gone,
Life anew around us all.
Back on Earth with noise and form,
The hustle bustle like days before.

You smile at me and me to thee,
Our smiles so bright for all to see.
A gift so precious given me and
You a gift so precious your life to be.

You smile at me I smile at you,
You laugh with me and I with you.
Our future bright as bright can be,
A flower you are and me the bee.

The day is bright and still and warm,
I hold you tight, live life's call! x

## 10. I cry for you tomorrow but Mamma I cannot stay

I cry for you tomorrow Mamma,
I cry for you I say.
I cry for you tomorrow Mamma,
I cry for you I pray.

I wave goodbye dear Mamma,
I wave goodbye can't stay.
I wave goodbye dear Mamma,
I wave I have to go away.

My wife you see she needs me,
My wife she does I pray.
My wife dear Mamma needs me strong,
I have work to do I say.

My wife she's hurt dear Mamma,
My wife needs me I pray.
Her heart is broken Mamma,
Have to go can't stay.

She's my love you see my Mamma,
My love you see I say.
You understand dear Mamma,
'I understand', I hear you say.

Love you so much dear Mamma,
Will love you more with each passing day,
But 'tis time I left dear Mamma,
Yes, time I have work to do I say.

'I love you too', says dear Mamma,
'Always have, always will', I hear you say,
A smile and kiss your gone dear Mamma,
But your love's here forever,
Forever here to stay.

I rush now dear Mamma,
I rush rush away,
My tears they wash all over me,
As thick as the oceans spray.

I rush now dear Mamma,
I rush to my wife I pray,
She needs me now dear Mamma,
I have work to do today.

The broken hearted lovebird,
I tend to you each day,
'Tis my pledge to you my lover,
I'm here for you I say.

I'll tend your broken heart song,
I'll sing to you each day,
I'll be strong, loving, steadfast,
My strength from me to you I pray.

I will bath your heart with my love,
Pray to angel's saints and say,
Give me strength and love aplenty,
For my lovebird needs this of me today.

I'll tend your broken heart song,
Through this windy stormy day,
The lightning I shall shield you from,
With my strong heart I pray.

My gentle touch comfort you, brush the tears from your face,
Gentle kisses to your forehead, cheeks, lips, I pray.

You shall fly again dear lovebird,
You shall fly again I say,
You shall fly my dearest lovebird,
Lean on me, take my strength, I pray. x

## 11. This day is so long

God stops time for us my love.
He holds the Sun up high my love.
It does not move nigh my love.
Behold the Sun so high my love.
This time for you and I my love.
The angels fuss they try my love.
Preparing night the same my love.
But He holds the Sun up high my love.
Just for you and I my love.
He holds the Sun up high my love.
Just for you and I my love.
My love and yours on fire my love.
Stoked by God's loving hand on high my love.
Just for you and I my love.
Our God does this on high my love.
Just for you and I my love.
Just for you and I my love. x

## 12. I cried a billion tears today

I cried a billion tears today,
From here to Heaven above I prayed.
For to God my Christ His Son I pray,
For to Him to let you stay one more day.

I cried and cried and cried some more,
Face awash they did adorn,
And then I cried a little more.

I did not know I could cry so much,
My heart my love you had so touched.
I cried and cried and cried some more,
My love for you my heart it tore,
To know of pain for you in store,
And I cried and cried even more.

I cried and cried and cried even more,
My face awash my breath rasped and raw.
The people they did a stop and stare and frowned,
Shaken forehead a nod 'look there!'

But I cried and cried I didn't care,
My love for you made raw laid bare,
For everyone to look to stare.
My love my love for you I cared.
For you I cried my soul laid bare. x

## 13. Only in time will I lose you

Only in time will I lose you,
Only forever have I sought you,
Only for eternity will I miss you,
Only with love have you blessed me. x

## 14. I have loved you my love. I have loved you!

I have loved you my love,
From here to Heaven above my love.

My heart has been yours only my love.

I cried when you found broken wing my love,
My heart torn apart my love.
I cried to Heaven above my love,
My tears drenched angel's wings my love,
Till they did fall sodden into your heart my love.

Did roar long hard my love,
To protect your tender heart my love.
I demanded sanctuary for thee my love,
That they be heralds for me my love,
To God in Heaven above my love.

Swiftly did they fly my love,
My tears falling from ahigh my love,
To bath my broken heart my love,
Torn and shredded heart my love,
Torn asunder apart my love.

It shriveled in the dark my love,
Your broken wing now torn apart my love,
Life's pain held you tight my love.

Nothing I could do my love,
To save you from the pain my love,
The awful awful pain my love.

The angels could not save my love,
Sheets of tears did they shed for you my love my love my love.

Where have you gone now my love?

The wind from Heaven above my love,
Has taken you away my love.

I awaken and you are gone my love,
I cry torrents to God above my love.
The oceans and mountains shrink from my wrath my love,
My shouts and screams echo through Heaven above my love.

I cannot stand the pain my love,
It is the eye of the storm my love,
Darkness covers me now my love,
I tremble and shake and howl my love,
I hunger and thirst for thee my love,
I have not eaten a thing my love,
For I only hunger for thee my love.

I want to be freed of such pain my love,
The darkness and the pain my love.
I miss you more than breath my love,
Our bed a sodden mess my love,
My tears my tears for thee my love my love.

I am a shriveled mess my love,
My thoughts of you in excess my love.
I cannot breathe my love,
I shall not breathe my love.

I have cried oceans of tears to Heaven above my love,
That the angels keep you safe my love.
With my tears that I did slake upon their wings my love,
They now do lovingly bathe your face my love.

My tears kiss your eyes, your lips, your face my love,
From me to you in Heaven above my love.

When will Heaven set me free my love?
To come and lay with thee my love,
In forests of verdant green my love,
With gentle soothing breeze my love,
Your touch to put me at ease my love,
Your touch to comfort me my love,
Your touch I miss of thee my love,
My heart my heart racked, it grieves my love.

Oh I miss thee my love,
Oh Heaven set me free my love,
I plead and plead to He my love,
Heaven set me free my love.

Soon I shall see thee my love,
Soon to be free my love,
To lay and hold thee my love,
For all eternity my love. x

## 15. A storm is coming

A storm is coming to take you my love,
A storm is coming from Heaven above.
A hurricane it is we know not when,
'Tis ferocious and fearsome that will not end.

A storm so great to take you away,
His storm of love His storm I pray.
For this storm my love is blinding of light,
It echo's forever with Heavens might.

My love for you darling cannot compare,
It pales in comparison to its blinding stare.
For this storm my darling 'tis God's love,
To ease your pain and suffering sent with his angel's from above.

For He has loved you my darling before time began,
For His love comes to take you back home again.
For His love my darling you should fear not,
For His love 'tis everlasting and shall never stop.

For His love my darling no man can dim,
For He has loved you even before time began.
I am flesh and blood but I know this is true,
I was sent to love thee as He loves you.

Throughout our lives you have given me your all,
Your strength your courage your love when I'd fall.
A storm is coming to take you home my love,
A storm is coming, back to Heaven above. x

## 16. This life is but a dream

This life is but a dream and I have dreamed it with you
And what a beautiful dream it has been my love. x

## 17. And you must toss all this away.

And you must toss all this away,
From this world she prayed.
I'll run from it today,
Let the ground cover me where I lay.

For here I shall not stay
But away on the wings of angel's I say.
Don't look away,
For I'll be gone today.
Don't blink I say,
For you'll miss my rising today.

Why can't she stay? I'd say,
Let me give my soul I prayed.
Not today not today,
You have work to do, she prayed.

So she smiled, closed her eyes and flew away that day.
And only the silence and I were left to pray.
All I know is I love you still I say.
Love you till I too can fly away. x

# 18. I sat there in the soothing breeze

I sat there in the soothing breeze,
By your side as you slept at ease.
The breeze it was not the same of old,
For this breeze it seemed to rush and hold,
Your breath so light and shallow drawn,
This breeze it seemed to you to hold.

A breeze of beating angel's wings,
Waiting for you to God to bring.
A breeze of vibrant singing chords,
Made up of God's angelic Lords.

Waiting, waiting for you to hold,
To take you back to his loving fold.
And with last breath this breeze did cease
And rushed away towards the east.
A rising sun, a brilliant dawn,
And with it my love you too were gone. x

## 19. I'm sorry you had to die.

I'm sorry you had to die Janey,
I'm sorry darling.
You know my heart now,
Always in it you shall be.

Why should I cry when I know you are safe with He,
Because I love, I love you Janey.

You are behind the veil of clouds, stars, moon and sun up high.
I stand on the cliff soon, then I too can fly.

Guide me as you have true,
For all my moments will always include you.

How many moons I don't know,
How many breaths till my last for you blows?

You smiled in the dream and said to me,
Live, love and pray for I am safe with He.

Hundreds of poems I have written now,
Each one for you 'tis how I bow.

To my dearest love, a life we lived and loved,
Rest peacefully darling with He above. x

## 20. There was nothing you could do

There was nothing you could do but show your love for others.
You found your peace,
As the sunshine baths a mountain warmly with the rising of
the sun.
Your heard His call and breathed a song of love to all.
You showed everyone how to live though you were leaving.

How desperate was our short time together.
You know my heart now,
It was all I could give you.

You are but a moments breath from me,
Rest now my love with the angels of eternity.
For forever will visit me one day
And to seek you once again is all I pray.

I will always miss you Janey girl.
I don't think I'll ever stop writing.
I will miss you till my last breath.
Your loving husband Renato x

## 21. As you danced my love

As you danced my love the stars fell to your feet,
'Alight us they called and we shall raise you to the Heavens.'
And your cloak had grown so so heavy my love.

'And with the washing of the rains of pain,
Shall come the light of the new dawn.'
As the blood of life ceased,
Only then did I hear God in the language of silence.
For his defining roar sung your name drowning my calls.

'Tear my flesh from my bones and scatter them to the four winds,
And a thousand times more.'
But I am here to finish my journey.

'Honour me by bringing light and love to others' and so I try.
'Honour me by living' and so I begin.
'Honour me for I am but a single breath from you my love.'
'And when you awake let it be to love.'
 And so all else ceased but love.
'Honour me for our love.'
And so I shall. x

## 22. You have not seen me cry

You have not seen me cry,
You have not seen my heart die.
I died with you that day,
I died with you I say.

My heart it died with your tears,
It died because with all your fears,
I could not save you my love my dear,
I could not save you from all those fears.

I could not save you, all I could do,
Was love you and love you and love you I prayed,
And love you and love you until that day,
We did part and love you still I do say.

I will love you till my dying day,
I will love you and love you 'tis all I can say,
I will love you and love you and love you more,
I will love you and love you of this you can be sure.

I did love you, still love you, will love you my love,
Will love you and love from me to you in Heaven above.

To all the angels and saints, I do say,
Take my love read its words to you I do pray.

Rest peacefully my love,
No more worries to break your heart,
Rest peacefully my love in the presence of God above.

Sit peacefully below the bull oak tree,
By the glistening running stream,
Spend your days in happiness and joy,
As you sit and wait for me.

May my time be swift my lovely Janey dear,
May my last heart's beat bring happiness to my ear.
For at that time again I shall hear,
Your loving voice whisper in my ear.

Come to me my love beneath the swaying bull oak tree,
Come to me my love lay softly with me here,
Hold me tight my love no more do you need to fear,
Kiss me gently my love from now to eternity. x

## 23. When I lost you

When I lost you all I asked for was peace,
'Tis all you wanted for me,
When we spoke that day before the drugs of haze took you.
'I'm going to miss you mate.' I said.
'I'm going to miss you too Ren, my husband and lover.'
'Promise me you won't grieve for too long though,'
'If you want to honour me,
Then do so by making other people feel good about themselves.'

'Why do you cry?' Asked the lovebird.
'Because I miss you.' He answered.
'Will you know where to travel.' Asked the lovebird.
'Yes you showed me how.' He answered.
'Then live, for I love you still and always will.'
'Will I tell others.' He asked.
'Only with love.' Answered the lovebird.

I live in a world of time though time ceased that day,
Each day I live for you with peace and happiness I pray,
One day I shall travel home of this I now am sure,
For I know you have prepared my welcome,

# The darkest dark

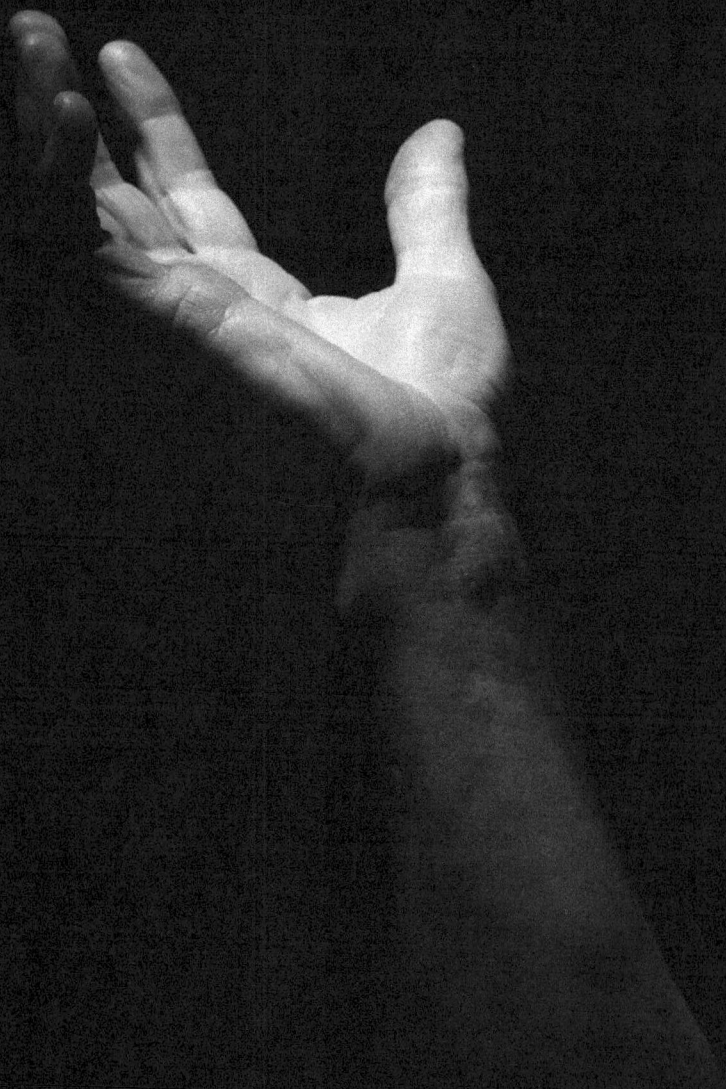

## 24. From our demons we run and hide

From our demons we run and hide,
For from their screams we cannot hide,
We run here, we run there,
For from such horror there is no compare.

There comes a time when we stand and face,
Our demon's taunts with loving grace,
Such bravery 'tis none compared,
To beauty of such battles where none are spared.

Such grace to see in painful eyes,
As you fight your battles day and night,
A witness to the grace in thee,
As you conquer demons in victory.

To stand breathlessly and wait for dawn,
A new chapter, the old ripped and torn,
I am man that does not kneel,
Except for God's love, which He gives to heal.

But now that I have seen His face,
Of conquered demons replaced by grace,
I kneel to you, for you are truly brave,
To have fought so long, with so much pain.

To have conquered night before glorious dawn,
As you now step forward from your terrible storm,
To face new life and all with grace,
With God's loving radiance upon your face.

Yes, I kneel to you for in you I see,
My battle too and my victory. x

( To the brave who battle to overcome their darkness x )

## 25. Fly my beautiful lovebird.

I held you my lovebird in the palm of my heart,
'Tis time beautiful lovebird for you to fly again from me to part,
I let you free to fly lovebird, fly high fly free,
Fly beautiful lovebird, fly high up to He.

Don't look back dearest lovebird, don't look back wild and free,
For my tears dearest lovebird are because I know you are free,
Oh fly beautiful lovebird, fly high fly free,
Oh my beautiful darling lovebird, always in my heart you shall be. x

## 26. Then tear at me

Then tear at me, rip at me, destroy me as I watch and stare,
Pound and crush me, flay and rush at me, as I lie here so aware,
My senses tingling, my chest a stinging,
For you slash at me with your screams of madness and echoes
of sadness.

'Stop it, leave meeeeee!' but you shall not,
For this the most terrible and lonely battle that no one else sees
or hears,
For during these nights left alone to face all my terrible
worries and fears,
For I scream and no one hears, so I scream and scream
and scream inside, as my soul runs and hides in tears,
For 'tis the bloodletting of painful sorrow after all these years.

So tear at me, rip at me, as I watch and stare,
For I battle myself in the darkness,
For any other terror, there is no compare.

# 27. Will you not hide from me in the dark.

Will you not hide from me in the dark?
And wait for my pain to part?
For the darkness now is my only friend,
The light too painful for you to send.

Into ruined heart torn in two,
Tossed aside trampled too,
This loss I endure too much to bear,
My love my love for you I care.

Of tortured words and tears am blind,
This savage world for me untwines,
As wave on wave my heart is lost,
To darkness now this life is tossed.

And now in darkness I do dwell,
My soul hidden from all this hell,
For my screams are not for this world,
For only angels can see my living hell.

I run from light, a tender touch,
Soft spoken words, such hurt too much.

Demons rummage through my heart,
Pillage and squabble for any worth,
They kick aside my lust for life,
Tear from it its very light.

For I am tossed and tossed and tossed,
For I search for you my love I've lost,
For this a cost I cannot pay,
And thus tears at my soul every day.

For in you I saw my life to be,
Not to end in tragedy,
I would tear and toss all I am aside,
To find a place for you to hide.

For we all lose this loss you bear,
For this world is never fair,
The world to me now naught to me,
Struck from my mind for all to see.

A fallen world we all are,
We search for God's love from afar.
For now I weep and wail and flay,
And pray to God with tears I pay,
That He love you and love you and love you more,
From now till eternities distant shore.

His angels made to love you too,
Mercy and compassion their lot construed,
To bath you with unfailing love,
As I scream to them up above.

I look to you with my hearts love eye,
And close my eyes to this world of fire,
They take my tears to you I pray,
To bath you lovingly wash all pain away.

My screams they tune to their love song,
And sing to you in unfailing throng,
Of massed immense multitude,
They bow to you for they love you,
As much as my love I truly do. x

## 28. The darkest dark.

How can the darkness be so dark and deeper still it becomes?
As a child who stands unknowingly this rushes and engulfs
you again,
So deep and so dark.

Even though you know the truth,
Even though your heart cannot escape it,
It's all consuming torture,
One quick breath and again under.

Rush as fast as you may from it,
But it waits for you in the darkness.
How black is this depth of loss?
How bitter sweet living becomes.

And so still my friend you spit out the sweetness of life,
Still your heart screams in the stillness of the deepest dark,
Still it wails and tortures you, engulfs you,
Tells you to leave this place.

How dark can darkness be?
Darker than the darkest of black sorrow,
Wishing each heartbeat was your last,
Wishing this veil of life would tear for you and set you free,
Wishing you were with her again.

So black, so dark, so painful.
How dark can the darkness be?
I miss you beyond this world,
Beyond this strife,
Beyond this breath,
Beyond my life.

## 29. I want to leave this world

I want to leave this world so much,
I want to rush from its painful grip,
I want to loosen its bony fingers upon my heart,
I want to stop breathing forever.

I want the light to be shut from me with a thud,
The darkness to cover me, cover me,
And cast me into the deepest pit,
Deeper still and again.

I am heartbroken, my heart is torn apart, tis true, it truly happens.
I bleed and less pains, the pains envelope me cover me,
Shut me off from this world,
No more light, ever ever.

My love why are you leaving me?
Why won't our God save you?

I cannot save you.
I am not a man, I am nothing, less than a worm, nay,
Nothing at all, less than the dust beneath my feet,
Nay, not even this but nothing,
Not a memory of this world even.

I cannot save you my love,
Forgive me, I am sorry, forgive me my love.

How can nothing write this?
It does not, it is the heckles of disdain and disgust,
Deriding, nothingness.

Let me walk amongst the living as if dead,
For I am dead, for I am nothing.


I would give you my life in half an eyes blink,
I would gladly with joy face the demons of hell for you.

We have stood in the fire together for so long my love,
The awful, awful fire.

I have laid upon the ground thrashing and gnawing,
Weeping for this not to be, not to be.

If it were not for our beautiful daughter my love,
I would come with you, on your last breath I would with joy,
Draw the knife into my heart swiftly,
So that I may lay with you my darling,
Believe me and know it is true, in an instant my love.

But you have asked me to stay here,
In this world naked without your love and alone,
So I must try, I must.

I shall not smile at the birds no more,
From their laughter I shall turn,
I shall cast my head down and walk away from joy in this world,
This it has been a stranger to me for so long and shall remain.

Every mirror shall shatter before me as my heart has,
The breeze shall part as it approaches me and not caress my brow,
Let flowers wilt before me,
And their pure sweet smells turn to putrid stench for me,
Let the sun stay hidden as I stumble in darkness,
Let me be mute to life's call.

I already miss you so so much,
It is like an unbelievable and endless terror,
I fall from the sky it is such a terrible terror.
The cliffs they beckon me they sneer at me,
They whisper to me to come closer, ever closer,
Such sweet bliss to stand at their edge,
I sweat being so close to you thus my love,
With one scraping step I could be with you,
Just one small step but my promise to you holds me
And pushes me back.

I will sing sweetly to you my love,
I shall think of you endlessly,
I shall set a place before me for you my love.

The storms they come and go as this one does,
As I know they must.
I close my eyes tight as the tears ooze
And think of your smiles and laughter,
I think of when we first met, of when we first kissed,
I remember it still beneath the she oak tree.
Of when we first made love.

And again the storms return.

Let my days here in this world rush away like an avalanche,
Let them tumble away so that I may quickly breath,
So I may reach my last breath,
I shall hold it for a while and smile with joy in my heart,
For I know that with its exhale,
The fogs of pain that separate us will be blown away,
And I will see you standing there,
Waiting for me beneath the she oak tree.

Always in my heart my love. x

# 30. The demons they rise again.

The demons they rise again,
They rise up in the night,
The demons they rise again,
They rise up with a fright.

They have returned again to me,
To taunt my weary heart,
They have returned again to me,
They stalk my gentle heart.

They rise up in the night time,
Through dim fog lit black haze,
They rise up in the night time,
Through the endless gnarling pain.

They rise up in the night time,
My heart misses beat again,
They rise up in the night time,
And I am lost to them again.

They come move on relentlessly,
They taunt and rally they rush,
They truly will devour me,
Tear open my tender heart.

My tears they issue forth,
My heart it wails and moans,
The demons do this thus to me,
Mouth pain upon their scorn.

My mind a bedazzled array of them,
Their taunts now hold me tight,
Their echoes pained inside my heart,
I awaken full of fright.

The sweat it bathes all over me,
I breath and then forget,
They taunt I should surrender to them,
My life I should forget.

I cry for angels, saints,
But no one hears my call,
I cry for them to save me,
So that I may not fall.

They move on relentlessly,
For my heart is full of fright,
They move on relentlessly,
Since I lost you my love that night.

# 31. Bashing crashing

Bashing crashing through life each day,
We bash and crash we fall may pray,
Stumble tumble scrape and swoon,
We falter tumble alone marooned.

We twist and turn and turn may pray,
Life it's black and blue and bright,
It's shut and dark,
So twisted may be straight.

I walked straight lined in view so true,
Then life's train it rammed too close and 'BAM,'
Now dark and dark and sharp with bite,
And bled I bleed bled dry sharp edged.

Screamed hell in ear no rest no sleep only fear,
Now dark in dark I bleed I scream,
Fire and ice and howling wind and sharpened claws on me
that gleam,
That dig and twist and gore and gnarl,
No peace no peace I scream I howl.

Love God still do,
Tested me through you,
Love God I do I do I do.

Rains now rains hard,
Rains now rains true.
Darkest hour before dawn you said,
Darkest hour 'tis drawn.


Silence now, silence now, darkest now, darkest dark.

I see no light no ray of bright,
Where art thou gone my brightest light,
Darkest dark no bright dawn,
Where are you gone? Where are you gone?

My heart is drawn and so I fall,
In silence dark I fall I fall,
But do not touch the ground at all.

I fall and fall and fall and fall,
Your hand holds me and then I stall,
Your hand holds me, rays of bright light then shine tall,
The wind dies no wind at all, your hand holds me I do not fall.

The dawn comes through dark it trawls,
The dawn it breaks standing tall,
A straight lined path in view so true,
A straight lined path from me to you.

My God, love God I cry still do,
Tested me He did my heart through you.
Calm soft grass tall trees gentle breeze,
Walk straight lined path now my God to you.

(Mamma died today. I love you always mia bella.)

## 32. The waves come by

The waves come by,
The waves come by,
They crash on heart,
They steal the light.

They thunder and roar,
They crash on by,
Thunder and roar,
They crash on by.

I am left standing wet with tears,
With all my fears that no one hears,
I am left wet with all my fears,
With all my fears that no one hears.

The waves they crash upon my heart,
My fears of future they do start,
A wailing sound in ear deep dread,
I hear death's voice inside my head.

The waves they crash,
And bash my heart,
My fears of future,
They do start.

The waves come by,
The waves come by.
They crash on heart,
They steal the light.

The waves come by,
The waves come by,
They crash on heart,
They steal the light.

## 33. I stumble in the darkness

I stumble in the darkness,
In the middle of the night,
For again my heart has left me,
It has screamed and taken flight.

For I awaken with a shudder,
In this world of pain and strife,
And wish I was no longer here,
If this be my wretched plight.

So I search thus empty hearted,
For that which I cannot strive,
To be with you my darling,
In a world of empty sights.

And so I stumble in the darkness,
In the middle of the night,
Hoping I am moving towards my awakening,
For that for me may one day dawn a breaking light.

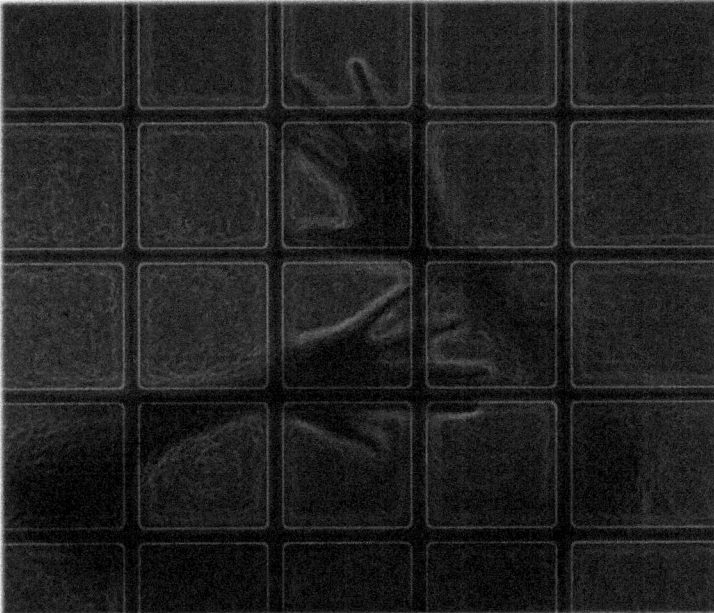

## 34. What it was of sadness spun.

What it was of sadness spun,
No one touched the caterpillar a life so glum,
And it set a place amongst the weeds,
A place to grieve it's pain you see.

During winters breath of sorrows storm,
It sat there still all forlorn,
Until the day when dawn did break,
And from it not a caterpillar did awake.

A new form woke upon springs breath,
The caterpillar from its form had left,
But a beautiful butterfly did alight,
From cocoon after dreaded night.

And still it's heart it was the same,
But turned it's grieving and all its pain,
For it now knew all to know,
And knew why it had to go.

For it now knew that all is love,
And it was ready to take flight above,
And on morning breeze it's wings did beat,
And took to Heaven wild and free.

And so it left upon this breeze,
For the light of love, it could see,
So it flew high up above,
To the place where there is only love,
To find its way home once again,
To live for eternity with its loving friend. x

## 35. The greatest battle I fought

The greatest battle I fought I strived,
I fought myself, just to stay alive.

For I have fought for so so long,
The screaming demons that would do me wrong.

For my battles you cannot see,
For they are fought in eternity.

But of one thing I am sure,
That such battles lead to Heaven's door.

For the battles I fight are with me,
They are the battles that separate us from He.

The greatest battle I fought I strived,
I fought myself, just to stay alive.

'Weeping may tarry for the night but joy comes with the morning'
(Psalm 30: 4-5-ESV)

# The missing

## 36. You speak to me through the leaves.

You speak to me through the leaves,
In the rustling of the beautiful trees.
You sing to me in your loving tune,
While I sit here in this world marooned.

The breeze that touches my tear draped face,
Like your warm caress your warm embrace.
The bird that sings in front of me,
'Tis you for now you have been set free.

The clouds that rush and wander by,
Are your chariots in the sky.
In sunshine bathed I feel your touch,
Your love for me I miss so much.

Rest now love in natures blessed,
Warm and soothing soft caress.
For in it you live in every way,
For eternity with God I pray. x

## 37. I saw the angels paint today

I saw the angels paint today,
For on the sky they had splayed,
A many splendid treat for you,
Composed of many varied hues.

A mixture of colours red and green,
And one's no earthly mortal has seen,
And as true beauty it did part,
But forever safe in one's loving heart.

So I was treated to His majesty
And it did bring a smile to me,
For I had left this world behind,
All restrictions of space and time,
To glimpse a moment of eternity,
That He has in store for you and me. x.

## 38. Why you had to fly.

Why you had to fly,
Why you had to die,
Why you left our love,
Rushed to Heaven above.

Miss you every day,
Wish you could have stayed,
Will love you till I die,
And begin my search up high. x

## 39. Where does the breeze blow?

Where does the breeze blow, I do not know?
It carries my whispers and dreams of you,
Listen carefully and you will hear,
Me whisper my love for you my dear. x

## 40. To see things a man should not see.

To see things a man should not see,
To know things a man should not know,
To hear desperation in the voice of the one you love,
All these things.

To hold on when life gives way,
To hold on when all that was is gone,
To love for love is all there is,
All these things.

To give for 'tis all you can do,
To wait for the rising of your new dawn,
To hold you to your last breath,
All these things. x

## 41. Love someone to their last breath.

Love someone to their last breath,
Love someone until there's nothing left,
Love someone till their day is done,
Love someone till from you they run,
Love someone till the last they see is you,
For in their eyes you shall see eternity too. x

## 42. I sing to you with wonder.

I sing to you with wonder,
I sing to you with love,
I sing to you my Father,
My God in Heaven above.

I send to you my lover,
I send to you my love,
I send to you my creator,
My wife to Heaven above.

Sing to her my Father,
Sing to her my love,
Sing to her for eternity,
With any eternity of love. x

# 43. I saw a butterfly in the rain

I saw a butterfly in the rain,
It settled on the windowpane,
The rain it battered tossed and bruised
But that little butterfly it did not move.

I held that butterfly in my hand,
Bruised and battered in so much pain,
Brushed the raindrops from its wings,
Into its heart my love I'd sing.

It then laid down upon my hand,
Its wings stop fluttering not even a sound,
Again the raindrops upon its frame,
My teardrops falling, I could not refrain.

I held that butterfly in my hand,
Loved it so much while it writhed in pain,
I hold that butterfly to my heart,
Now it is safe forever never to part. x

## 44. I have hidden you deep in my heart love.

I have hidden you deep in my heart love,
Where no one knows where to go,
I will visit you there in my dreams,
Where the she oaks sway to and fro.

You sit with Him quietly,
By the sun dappled green grassed brook,
You speak to Him in your silence,
For this is the language He took.

An eternity He has loved you,
Before the stars and sky He made,
His loving heart longing,
To see you once again.

My veil of tears in this life,
Are all that keep me here,
For my love I grieve for you,
For it seems like an eternity.

Sit quietly with Him now love,
For the only thing in this life I'm sure,
With his kindness and compassion,
He will lead you to Heaven's door.

No more worries and pain for you love,
These things have past apart,
For He sits with you with endless compassion,
Showering endless mercies upon your heart.

An eternity He has waited,
With His loving angels too,
For they also were made to love you,
For eternity 'tis true.

For they now as forever,
Wait patiently at Heaven's door,
He will lead you there my darling,
To this far off distant shore.

I have hidden you deep in my heart love,
Where no one knows where to go,
I will visit you there in my dreams,
Where the she oaks sway to and fro. x

## 45. Just how much I loved you.

Just how much I loved you,
No one will ever know,
What it meant to lose you,
To this day the angels wail and moan.

For in this world of riches,
I would give it all away,
To see your smiling face again,
'Tis all to him I pray. x

## 46. I shall take my sadness put it to sleep

I shall take my sadness put it to sleep,
For you have known of sorrow for years did weep,
For the land of sorrow knows not time,
No reason no logic no cure no rhyme.

When time stood still on that desperate night,
All my fears betrayed me felt all hope take flight,
The horror, desperation, devastation and loss,
As if you yourself were on that cross.

But it all did part and in its place,
The face of sorrow I have traced,
With trembling fingers, a heart that bleeds,
The face of sorrow, that shall always grieve. x

## 47. For sorrow is a ruler that has no king.

For sorrow is a ruler that has no king,
The true deceiver that lies within,
For it brings to you your mortality,
But also you yearn to be set free.

I will always love you for me now time stands still,
For sorrow robbed us of our fill,
Now there is no fear left in me,
Just the hidden tears for you my dear.

My heart shall always echo your final breath,
For with it part of my soul from me it fled,
To search for you in eternity,
And when found back to me to set me free. x

# 48. I miss you

I miss you.

These are the three words I will utter for the rest of my days.
I miss the love we shared,
But more than that, what our souls shared.
For how I miss you goes beyond this world and this life.

I miss your presence,
I miss you.
I miss your soul,
For I know my soul will always miss you.

In the darkness of the night,
In the morning light,
I miss you.

I talk to you because you asked me to.
I miss you.

I listen for you and shall hear you in my last breath.

I miss you,
I miss you,
I miss you. x

## 49. And I shall wait for you.

And I shall wait for you till the sun goes down,
I shall wait for you till I am wrinkled and brown,
I shall wait for you till I forget my name,
Or what I wrote, or how you kissed without blame.

I shall wait for you till I've nothing left,
Till this world has stolen all my memories blessed,
I shall wait for you till my last breath leaves,
For as I promised it is for you that breeze.

I shall wait for a while, while I slumber deep,
In the darkest pit, no sound no squeak,
And when I awake, I shall wait no more,
For there you shall be, as you were before. x

## 50. And in time the grass grew

And in time the grass grew lovers breathed as life bloomed,
But I was left my heart marooned,
For forever shall my heart mourn,
What we lost our futures dawn.

Now I wait 'tis all I do,
For the day I shall again see you,
I am broken torn in two,
For you see my love half of me left with you.

So forever in this world I shall grieve,
Till my breath this world it leaves,
To lay with you upon our shore,
To wait for Christ, the one adored. x

## 51. I shall miss you forever in the depths of my heart.

I shall miss you forever in the depths of my heart,
I shall miss you forever that night that broke my heart,
I shall miss you forever since the angels took you home,
I shall miss you forever for now I wander here alone.

I shall miss you forever for I also died inside,
I shall miss you forever for all the pain that you did hide,
I shall miss you forever for in forever I shall see,
When the angels come to call I shall search for you in eternity. x

## 52. You have hidden the treasure within my heart

You have hidden the treasure within my heart,
You placed it there with grace and mercy the night you left,
Given to you by He.

It was and shall always be,
The priceless gift I shall treasure my love.

For all that is unseen I have seen.
All that men fear I fear not.
All that was silence now sings within my heart.
When the butterfly lands,
I remember it's life as our few weeks together.

When the breeze blows, I am sure I shall one day follow.
When the sun sets, I know through Christ it has risen for you.

## 53. I faced the loss of my love last night.

I faced the loss of my love last night,
In the early morning I woke my heart affright,
I whispered to myself in the cool crisp air,
What I had avoided till now that which I could just not bear.

I whispered the words my heart had not heard,
I whispered them gently as my eyes did burn,
I whispered them just as a lover would,
To the one he loves so they shall not be misunderstood.

I whispered them clear as this night had become,
My heart transfixed no longer to run,
I whispered them sweet as fresh fallen rain,
I whispered them like medicine that washes away pain.

I whispered the words, 'Goodbye my love,
Rest peacefully with God now in Heaven above.'
Yes, I whispered those words just once and never again,
Until my soul to Heaven He sends. x

## 54. I did what I thought I could not do.

I did what I thought I could not do,
For you faced death and I held true,
I lead you where the darkness fell,
And was your lamppost as you past through hell.

My presence fixed for I could see,
On your last breath you would be free,
I still hold true you now do sleep,
For His grace in you still makes me weep.

I sing with praise and tears in eyes,
Since that day my love you died,
For on His day you will rise again,
And until that day my love to you I send. x

## 55. 'Where have you gone my lovebird?'

Where have you gone my lovebird,
To the depths of my heart,
For in losing you my lovebird,
All my worries they did start.

For it 'twas true my darling lovebird,
In this world there is nothing more,
Than the love He has given freely,
To lead us back to His loving door.

For all that matters,
'Twas given from His heart unrefrained,
An abundance of His love,
To lead us home once again.

For in losing you my lovebird,
Only now can I see,
The immensity of His love,
Has been abundantly made clear.

The sole purpose of one's life,
Is to love and nothing more,
For only this is the key to our heart's,
That will lead us back to Him restored.

So love all around you,
And in each moment find His grace,
For only then truly lovebird,
In such moments shall I see your face.

So I shall love my beautiful lovebird,
In this world gone astray,
And in doing so in each moment,
Move ever closer back to you once again.

For my last breath is yours and yours alone,
This I promised you my love,
Remember it was witnessed,
By all the angels in Heaven above.

So let me love it's all that matters,
It's all that will ever be,
From now this beautiful moment,
Until eternity.

So love and love again,
And love even more,
Till the day 'tis time for my last breath,
For you my lovebird the one I adore. x

## 56. 'Where have you been?' Asked the lovebird.

'Where have you been?' Asked the lovebird.
'I have been in the storm that has washed me clean,
In the land of sorrow sight unseen.'

'And where will you go?' Asked the lovebird.
'Wherever my heart will lead me,
Whatever life's fortunes bestows,
For I have tortured myself for years now,
For now it is time to grow.'

'But how will you know?' Asked the lovebird.
'My heart will answer me true,
With kindness and love in memory of you.'

'What will you see?' Asked the lovebird.
'Only love from God,
Reflected in me.'

'How will you stand?' Asked the lovebird.
'Graciously and courageously,
If it is His plan.'

'How will you love?' Asked the lovebird.
'With all my heart and soul,
As 'twas ordained by God above.'

'How will you sing?' Asked the lovebird.
'With joy and love,
Flowing within.'

'And on your last breath what shall you do?' Asked the lovebird.
'Smile with gladness knowing,
I have lived a good life, in memory of you.' x

## 57. One day I shall leave this place.

One day I shall leave this place,
One day I shall disappear like the wind,
One day my name will be lost,
One day I will lay with the dust,
One day, He shall shake the Heavens with a shout. x

## 58. For I have seen

For I have seen the beauty in every breath. x

## 59. And almost now the day is done.

And almost now the day is done,
Almost now two years have come,
Since the night your soul took flight,
Since the night my world became fright.

And so I miss you as much and more,
And so I'll miss you till Heaven's door,
When my day too shall become the night,
And my soul too from flesh takes flight.

To make its way to the dawn He sends,
To make its way back home again. x

## 60. He took you to a time of the setting of the sun.

He took you to a time of the setting of the sun,
You watched in awe of splendor, as His miracle was undone,
He placed love deep within you, as He took all that you cared,
For in losing the true value of this life, you have been made aware.

In a moments breath reality changed for me for evermore,
As You took my love led her with loving angels to Heaven's door,
For this life's sole purpose is to love and be loved as He ordained,
'Tis a purpose that no living soul, should ever from refrain. x

Renato Petronio

# The dawn comes

## 61. My heart is now closed to the darkness

My heart is now closed to the dark,
No more darkness anymore,
I begin to breathe again, to live again, to be somewhat happy,
To see the sun again, to breath the fragrance of life,
After so much darkness, after such a long, long night,
I see the sun rising, the dawn breaking.

I draw the deepest, deepest breath, after having held it for so long,
Stretching and yawning after this long night.
T'is true, it is darkest before the brightest dawn,
So now mine breaks, my dawn now awakens.

I seek now my souls thirst to slake,
For everything is in this moment of silence as the dawn rises,
Everything of any worth is in this silence of sunrise.

So I can smile again,
So I can love again,
So I can live again,
So I can give again,
So I have learnt of my heart,
So the secrets are mine to give,
So in losing you, I have gained truth.

So what is of worth then and only it.

So I breath again, yes I breath again.
Look, what a beautiful, beautiful sunrise. x

## 62. If you can sit with His silence.

If you can sit with His silence,
In your heart still,
Then you know you are ready,
You have taken your fill.

Of the pain and the sorrow,
That has come from days past,
That has tortured your soul,
And forever to last.

For the time for new growth,
Has come from within,
And the soil of your soul,
Sodden to brim.

New growth of life,
Of beauty anew,
Know that I will always love you,
That my love is true. x

## 63. And the wind shall blow and blow away.

And the wind shall blow and blow away,
For 'tis a new summers day,
Washed and cleansed clean away,
The wind shall blow the clouds away.

The silent heart with Him I pray,
Gone from this world with Love to stay,
The wind it tore ferociously,
From my grasp you were taken and were set free.

Now the breeze blows softly on this summer's day,
Blows softly my prayers to Him it takes,
The breeze surrounds you gently I pray,
Envelopes you for through Him darling you are saved. x

## 64. My darkest hour has come and gone.

My darkest hour has come and gone,
And with it the raging terrible storm,
A fresh landscape awaits Your grace,
For wondrous new life to fully embrace.

A new dawn breaks upon the shore,
A magnificent brightness of heart restored,
And with it joy of wondrous delight,
For new life's joy, for new life's bright.

To free the souls of those in pain,
With love and mercy unrefrained,
'Twas given freely in my hour of need,
So shall I give now to those that bleed.

For they had looked and saw with heart,
That did not flinch turn away or part,
For in their heart was gifted them,
The gift of love to heal and mend. x

## 65. I'm free, free of this world.

I'm free, free of this world,
Free, my future unfurled,
Free for I have conquered my fear,
Free for a future I see so dear.

Free of the darkness and the pain,
Free to breath and live again,
I'm free, for I've not been for so long,
Yes, I'm free, I'm free to live again.

Free from time, free from space,
Free to wander eternities blessed place,
I'm free for in my heart I know,
On my last breath eternity He shall bestow. x

# 66. You have freed me from this world.

You have freed me from this world,
All its troubles now unfurled,
And through time we both did see,
What true love could truly be.

No more worries now my love,
For you are safe with He above,
I must now walk here all alone,
With mercy and compassion as my home.

For all my troubles have faded away,
Since the moment I lost you that day,
I can smile and laugh now true,
Knowing one day again I'll be with you. x

## 67. And what was sorrow and what was pain.

And what was sorrow and what was pain,
Now a shower or far of rain,
And what was death my place to rest,
Now is life oh so blessed.

And what was grief the screams of night,
Now is morning beauty bright,
And what were tears that from heart rolled,
Now do angels tenderly bath your soul.

For I will miss you till my last breath,
When only with love I am left. x

## 68. I can see my heart now.

I can see my heart now, for He allowed me to glimpse eternity.

On that night He shone the star so bright,
All my worries and fears vanished took flight,
For He allowed me to glimpse eternity,
Where now my love forever shall be.

Safe and joyous and never the night,
That still visits me but without the fright,
For now I can sit in the darkest dark,
And remember the star that wonderful spark,
That ignited in me the moment of truth,
That is given with love to me and you.

So now the darkness is dark no more,
For I have seen what He has in store,
And it is only love for all shall cease,
And what shall be left is love for you and me. x

## 69. Your hearts love shall guide you home.

Your hearts love shall guide you home,
Your soul shall light the way,
I live that truthfully in your memory,
And to Him always shall I pray. x

## 70. Let the weight of this world.

Let the weight of this world leave you,
Let it wash away as dew,
As the morning sun that greets you,
As the mornings love holds you.

Let the morning breeze that surrounds you,
Brush the cobwebs that have taken hold,
For remember the words I told you,
Given to us from God foretold.

'My love will never leave you,'
'My love will never fold,'
'For My love 'tis everlasting,'
'For with My love I made your souls,'

'I shall bath her heart with mercy,'
'For dear to me her name I hold,'
'To you I promise this kindness,'
'That the day I come to call,'

'She shall rise again through His grace,'
'She shall rise for you to hold,'
'She shall rise to life everlasting,'
'She shall rise the day He calls.' x

## 71. With all the pain and suffering that has come.

With all pain and suffering that has come,
We surely should have come undone,
But love and mercy showered free,
Our broken hearts that did so bleed.

And so with love we travelled through,
The valley dark with friends so true,
To claim the prize that He gives free,
He rose and gave unto thee.

The chariot of the sky He gave to you,
My love you were so brave so true,
And with His angels you did ride,
To His paradise in the sky.

The angels now sit with you my love,
And smile at your beauty now above,
In awe they seek you every day,
Such grace displayed till taken away,
So sit and tell your tales of love,
And how you found Christ who you did love. x

## 72. When you bring beauty to others.

When you bring beauty to others,
So do you bring beauty to your own heart,
When you touch beauty in others,
So shall beauty touch your own heart.

When you sing beauty to others,
So shall its beautiful birdsong sing to one's heart,
When beauty is opened,
It shall flow unendingly like a rushing stream.

Light beauty in others,
For it shall light even the darkest night,
with the most brilliant light. x

# The light

## 73. If you knew the truth what would you do?

If you knew the truth what would you do?
Tell the whole world let them ridicule you?
If you saw the light shining so bright,
Would you open your heart or become like the night?

If He showed you the star what would you need?
Nothing of this world that has made us both bleed,
If you had the key where would you go?
Away to your dreams that lead the way home. x

## 74. I give you back to God now.

I give you back to God now,
I give you back to Love,
For you see like me He has loved you,
But for an eternity in Heaven above.

He stood above our forms thus,
And showered our hearts with love,
His angels sang to our hearts,
As He made us in Heaven above.

Before time and space He has loved you,
Before oceans and mountains were made,
An eternity He has loved you,
Longing to hold you once again.

I give you back to God now,
To love you once again,
For His love 'tis everlasting,
For His love shall never fail. x

## 75. I sit here silent, dark all alone.

I sit here silent, dark all alone,
Just a moment's breath from my eternal home,
With the sickness that tears at my flesh,
With eternal life I shall be blessed.

The pain and suffering that racks my bones,
Tell me it's time for You to take me home,
As my hair falls from my head,
To make way for the crown that You will set.

As strength ebbs from my sight,
Your Grace and Mercy on me alight,
And tears awash upon my cheek,
A testimony of love safe angels shall keep.

For as my eyes grow weary and dim,
Your everlasting Love shall shine within,
For You are Love and Love alone,
So come oh Love, for at last take me home. x

## 76. I fight with demons in my heart.

I fight with demons in my heart,
'Tis love they battle try to make it part,
Try to conquer all that is good and kind,
Try to render love to the passage of time.

But 'tis You I see now in all of this,
'Tis You I see through this world's mist,
'Tis You I see the Man of Sorrows,
'Tis You I see my hope of tomorrow.

For You were there in my dark,
For You were Love that did not part,
You were God come as man,
Died our death as was His plan.

Rose was raised from the dead,
You my God for me you bled,
So you see it is You I see,
Now, tomorrow, till eternity. x

## 77. I have faced my greatest fears and survived.

I have faced my greatest fears and survived,
I have cried an ocean of tears and am still alive,
The darkness I have dwelt no man should see,
For I have peered into the depths of eternity.

Having stood at the door of hell,
Having heard its terrible bell,
Having known of this world's loss,
Her having paid the ultimate cost.

Having known more than a man should bear,
Having looked into the eye of deaths stare,
I have faced all this worlds loss,
And the only thing I now know is His loving cross.

For He came to me when all was lost,
When all this world was lost to fright,
He came to me a star bright light,

I will never stop writing of He,
For His cross shone bright that night for me,
To tell me it was OK to breath,
That she was now safe for eternity.

The greatest peace He could have given me,
That He loves us all for eternity. x

## 78. My will is still it has raged its fill.

My will is still,
It has raged its fill,
Of fearsome shadows and demons shrill,
That of my soul set out to kill.

In time their flaying jagged claws,
Blunted by the love in me restored,
I stared in secret blessed places unknown to them,
My mercies and love they did not bend.

Until from me their taunts did still,
And ran from me having had their fill,
For in silence they had cut my heart,
But now in silence His strength did start.

For 'tis the language that He took,
And taught me from His loving book,
So now the demons they are no more,
From me they ran my soul restored.

For His angels guide my words from above,
Of peace, mercy, grace and love. x

## 79. The leaves have fallen.

The leaves have fallen thick to cover the forest floor,
Leaf after leaf after leaf until I can see no more,
'Tis time now I bent my back,
To reclaim my life from sorrows trap.

And if the sun does not shine,
Then rise above the clouds to reclaim what is mine,
I leave this place now where I have stood waiting for your return,
Where my heart has been calling as it burns.

What my mind knows my heart did not,
Till this very moment it did stop,
Knowing that from me you are gone,
After all the tears I have dropped.

So I shall set myself alight,
Like a phoenix in the night,
I shall burn brighter than the brightest sun,
And with light rising a new day dawn.

I shall rise high above the clouds and wave goodbye,
And float away to where I know not why,
No more darkness for me to see,
Only peace and happiness I'll breath.

I seek on high to be free,
I shall hide you in my heart as we fly,
And fly high into the beautiful sky,
Only smiles for you now my love.

Only love for enough have I died,
Goodbye my darling the winds rush by,
Goodbye my love, goodbye, goodbye,
'Tis time for me again to fly. x

# 80. What will you love when all this is gone?

What will you love when all this is gone?
Torn away by this world's terrible storm,
Where will you pray when darkness surrounds?
Neither movement, touch nor a memory abounds.

Who of this world will save your soul?
When your flesh is torn bones crumble and fall,
Who shall you call to on your very last breath?
When this world fades away and there is nothing left.

For I tell you there is one and one man alone,
Who died for our sins was buried behind stone,
And on the third day He rose from the dead,
Conquered sin, hell and finally death.

Only in this man lies all of our hope,
For mercy and love is of what He spoke,
So leave this world behind and seek His grace,
The eternity of love that lights His face.

For He is The Lord Jesus Christ, King of Kings,
To Him one day all the world shall sing,
The redeemer, the saviour, the truth, the light,
For through Him is our beautiful future bright.

Who of this world will save your soul?
When your flesh is torn bones crumble and fall,
Who shall you call to on your very last breath?
When this world fades away and there is nothing left. x

## 81. He is always there.

He is always there in the darkness of the night,
He is always there with the breaking of the light,
He is always there in the driving of the storm,
He is always there in the beauty of the morn.

He is always there when my heart has taken fright,
He is always there with His courage and His might,
He will be there when my last breath is given free,
He will be there too, to lead me home, set me free. x

## 82. As a flower you give unceasingly.

As a flower you give unceasingly,
The fragrance of your scent,
As a stream you flow unendingly,
Towards wounded hearts to mend.

A lover loves not flesh and blood,
But souls each rapturous breath,
To fill each open wounded hole,
With loving sensuous breath.

You are love, for love loves love alone,
As love can only love,
For love 'tis said is given free,
From Love from God above. x

## 83. And what was love shall always be.

And what was love shall always be,
Now until eternity,
For He shall come with Truth and Light,
And with Loves sword death shall smite.

For He did come and for us did bend,
Was sent to Sheol by God and then,
Conquered sin, banished death,
Brought salvation when naught was left.

For He is Lord, for He is King,
For Lord Jesus Christ all voices shall sing,
My Lord, my Christ, my peace of High,
Because of You I shall one day rise. x

## 84. Oh so much darkness I have felt.

Oh So much darkness I have felt,
For in the darkness having dwelt,
My soul in turn became the sun,
No longer from the darkness runs.

For having dwelt in desperate depths,
And from insanity a moment's breath,
It learnt to live and love again,
And rise afresh for its love it sends, to all it meets until time's end.

For only light does it now see,
For He sent the star from eternity,
And breathed new life again in me,
Saved me from insanity, for love now is all I see,
Until the day eternity, shall visit again my last breath in me.

For I confess that I love He,
The one that chased the darkness from me,
Shall love Him for eternity,
Shall love Him, for He set me free. x

# Only love

## 85. There are no more mysteries left to tell.

There are no more mysteries left to tell,
For all I have seen I have shared as well,
All the beauty and grace of my loving wife,
All our troubles our worries and her loss of life.

For I know she is safe and there is nothing to fear,
For when I called her name her angels appeared,
And showed me His Love He has for her,
Showed me His love for all to share. x

## 86. To our dearest daughter.

We stood there smiling mum and me,
Now with you in our arms our baby had become three.
Your eyes as blue as sapphires,
Your hair of angel white,
Your skin fresh fallen snowflakes,
Your heart with ours tonight.

You smiled at us our baby,
Our hearts they missed a beat,
For this our God had made us,
Our love now so complete.

Know that we are always with you,
Through sunshine storm and gale,
Our love 'tis everlasting,
Our love will never fail.

Our beating hearts intertwined now,
Our hearts made into one,
For this we had been made thus,
You our blessing from God above.

We are born to love and be loved,
Of this I can be sure,
Both mum and I we love you,
From now to evermore.

You stand now a grown beautiful woman,
Stand tall confident and proud,
But always do remember,
To be kind to all around.

You are our arrow we shoot now,
Into futures far away,
But remember we will always love you,
Since the day we held our babe. xxoo

## 87. Goodbye my love.

Her eyes slowly fluttered open, the streaming light that filled them was different, like the feeling you get before opening a present during Christmas. She raised herself onto one elbow and looked about, it's then she realised what had happened and where she was.

A smile as wide as the unsearchable sun broke across her face and she started laughing, laughing and laughing with her head tossed back, her beautiful hair flowed over her. She thought she would never stop and well it wouldn't have mattered if she didn't, for she had forever to laugh now, forever to love, forever and ever.

She rose and stood there, no pain, no pain! A rush of breath filled her lungs and she threw her arms high and continued to laugh as she started to run through the endless field of flowers, crimson yellow pink, all colours.

A fragrance filled her senses, not of the flowers but purely intoxicating and numbing at the same time. She stopped running for she felt a presence, she began to ever so slowly turn, as lovers first do when they first embrace and there He stood, so beautiful, so magnificent, yet so humble. He smiled and opened His arms to her as she ran to Him. She had come home, home at last, forever home. xo

## 88. God has written secret mysteries.

God has written secret mysteries upon my heart,
Your love for me is the greatest of these. x

## 89. Love sings endlessly to my heart.

Love sings endlessly to my heart,
For whatever my soul needs to do, it is ready. x

Always in my heart my love. x

## 90. 'So you did what you wanted?'

'So you did what you wanted?' Asked the lovebird.
'Yes.' He answered.
'So what now?' Asked the lovebird.
'I shall love, for the only truth is love.' He answered.
'Then there shall be no more night?' Asked the lovebird.
'No.' He answered, smiling.
The lovebird smiled back and said,
'I will not return again till we awake.'
He smiled and gently kissed her one last time.
The lovebird flew high into the sky,
Till she was but a shimmer of sunlight.
'Till we awake then.' he whispered smiling,
As she disappeared into the heavens. x

John 16:33
'I have told you these things,
so that in me you may have peace.
In this world you will have trouble. But take heart!
I have overcome the world.'

www.ingramcontent.com/pod-product-compliance
Lightning Source LLC
Chambersburg PA
CBHW070635030426
42337CB00020B/4021